Separation Anxiety

Leaving Dogs Home Alone

Chad Culp

This book is dedicated to

My wife, Dawn and our dogs
Jackson, Missy & Nakita

Separation Anxiety

CONTENTS

Separation Anxiety

PREFACE

Dogs left alone and unsupervised can wreak havoc on homes and gardens. I've seen couches and carpets destroyed, door frames chewed to pieces, sheetrock eaten through, sprinkler systems ripped from the ground, car interiors torn to shreds....you name it. And this is just the damage to property. What about the noise these uneasy dogs can make? Screams of pain and anguish coming from your home the likes of which the world has never known. Animal welfare groups come pounding on the door, "Excuse me, but we've received some complaints about animal abuse at this address. Do you mind if we have a look around?" How embarrassing!

Seriously though, people do get embarrassed and neighbors can file complaints, but worse than all of the destruction and strange looks from the family living next door is the strong likelihood that dogs may actually injure themselves. The desperate attempts dogs make to escape often result in grief, guilt and, yes, even vet bills.

"What in the world is going on with these dogs?"

It could be Separation Anxiety.

Separation Anxiety: noun

sep·a·ra·tion anx·i·e·ty

A form of anxiety experienced by a young child and caused by separation from a significant nurturant figure (and typically a parent) or from familiar surroundings. *Merriam-Webster*

As a Certified Professional Dog Trainer and Behavior Consultant, I would add to the definition above and say that it is not limited to humans. Dogs can also suffer from separation anxiety and more frequently than you might think.

At any given time, I can take a look at my upcoming appointments to find that nearly

25% of the humans requesting my training services have, or at least think they have, a dog with separation anxiety. That's one out of four dogs on my schedule! Holy smokes! Can it really be that much of an epidemic? Perhaps, but keep in mind that not all noisy or destructive behavior exhibited by dogs is due to separation anxiety. In reality, only about half the people I see who think they have a case of separation anxiety on their hands actually do, but that is still more than one in ten clients, and definitely enough to warrant some attention.

This book is designed to help you figure out if your dog actually does have separation anxiety and, if so, what you can do to get your dog to feel better about being home alone.

CHAPTER 1 - HOW TO USE THIS BOOK

As a Certified Professional Dog Trainer and Behavior Consultant, my days are spent helping people and their dogs in person. With the growth of the internet and social networking I am now getting requests for advice on dealing with separation anxiety from all over the world. I know we live in a world of sound bites, but trying to remedy this serious behavior issue with Tweets, Blogs and Facebook posts simply won't cut it. So, I decided to write something extensive and comprehensive enough to help people, no matter where they might live, prevent or resolve separation anxiety in their dogs.

This book is organized into three main categories:

- Symptoms

- Causes

- Solutions

It is designed to be read from start to finish. Some of the messages and concepts will be repeated and any redundancy is intentional, but as you go through the book, it will also be assumed that you have read the previous sections. The ideas build on each other, so please try to avoid the temptation to skip ahead or take short cuts.

I would also recommend taking notes as you go along, bookmark important pages and highlight important phrases or sections. In the Summary, I have incorporated a "Quick-View Recap" of important points which you can compare or compile with your own notes.

As you read, you'll notice the use of he or she in reference to dogs. This is because I don't like to use the term "it" when referring to a dog, even though my spell check software wants me to. I alternate between he and she just to make sure neither gender feels left out. I also alternate between your dog and the dog because some readers may be dealing with their own dog and others may be working with a dog that is not their own.

I hope you and your dog find all the solutions you need within these pages.

CHAPTER 2 – SYMPTOMS: RECOGNIZING SEPARATION ANXIETY

Many of the humans I see on a daily basis think their dog has separation anxiety, but, in truth, many of these dogs are just bored, lacking leadership or haven't been taught basic manners. Just because a dog barks, digs, or tries to escape does not mean he has separation anxiety. If a dog truly has separation anxiety he will be in an actual state of fear or panic when left alone.

If you are unsure or think your dog may have separation anxiety this section will help you recognize which symptoms are truly indicative of this behavior.

Physical Signs of Anxiety

The following behaviors will start the moment you leave and will continue until you return.

The dog will show immediate signs of being stressed, anxious or panicked. Panting, drooling and pacing are typical signs that are easily recognizable. These symptoms can even start as soon as the dog picks up on clues that you are getting ready to leave such as blow drying your hair or grabbing the car keys. These are what behaviorists call triggers. Dogs are excellent at picking up on human behavior patterns, especially dogs with separation anxiety, since they are always nearby and always watching. Which bring us to another symptom...

Shadowing

Dogs with separation anxiety follow their humans like a shadow. They need to constantly be in the same room and usually within a few feet of their owners. I have had many clients who can't even go to the bathroom without the dog going with them.

Vocalization & Destruction

This is a biggy! Barking, digging, whining, howling, scratching at doors, chewing and pretty much all manner of noise and destruction are present in separation anxiety cases. Most of the calls I get for separation anxiety come because the dog has caused some sort of damage to property or rattled some nerves and tested human ear drums. Let's face it, if they didn't, most people wouldn't think it was much of a problem and would probably not be looking for help. In other words, if you're reading this, your dog has probably already damaged something of value to you, hurt himself, gotten on your nerves or the neighbors have complained about the noise.

Note to trainers: You may be reading this because you're a trainer or behaviorist looking for some fresh tips in which case you already know what I'm talking about. If you're a new trainer, then just expect that these types of concerns or complaints will be the case with most of the calls you get regarding separation anxiety. Be prepared to consult a person who is frazzled, upset, emotional and possibly even on the verge of getting rid of the dog. Be patient and understanding with these dog owners. It's just human nature to act as if nothing's a problem until it's a problem for us. Until it impacts us directly in some way, particularly our wallet, we tend to procrastinate. You are probably guilty of this yourself. Maybe not with your dog but probably in some other aspect of your life, so be nice to your clients and try not to upset them. Seriously, many will be on the verge of tears already and lecturing them won't help. You can't go back in time, so just help them move forward.

The savvier dog owner will understand the importance of prevention and look for help at the early stages, but this is the exception, not the norm. Most people will not notice the early signs or think the dog will eventually "grow out of it." It's not until things get out of control that they will finally look for, ask for and be willing to pay for help.

Frantic Escape Efforts

Intensely pawing, scratching, chewing and digging to escape the house, kennel or yard is typically seen in dogs with separation anxiety. In extreme cases these efforts will be frantic, often times leading to injury. These efforts will happen only when alone and most likely every time they are left alone.

If a dog tries to escape, but only occasionally, he may just be bored or there may be a female in heat or there could be any number of other reasons for making an escape. The Fourth of July, New Year's Eve and thunderstorms are common times for frantic escape efforts due to fear of uncommon noises and commotion. In these cases, while it may not be true separation anxiety at the outset, if being left alone becomes associated with the fear they experienced from the noise, separation anxiety can be the end result.

Relieving In the House

Dogs that are otherwise housebroken may relieve themselves in the house but only when left alone. The key phrase here is otherwise housebroken. If the dog also has accidents in the house when the owners are home, then this cannot be considered a sign of separation anxiety. In that case, the dog is simply not fully housebroken yet.

Frenzied Greetings

Most dogs are excited to see their owners when they come home and most owners will say that that's one of the great things about having dogs. I hear humans defend the excited greetings their dogs give them all the time. It goes something like, "It's wonderful to have that kind of love in your life and to be greeted so warmly, isn't it?" Dogs with separation anxiety, however, will take this concept to a whole new level. They will give beyond the typical excited greeting and will achieve a new level of frenzied emotion, even if the owners were only gone for a few minutes.

Hunger Strike

Many dogs will not eat or drink when left alone. Refusal of food or water is common in a dog that is stressed. This can be seen in dogs that are afraid of people, dogs, loud noises and various environmental or situational stressors. For some dogs, being left alone is one of those stressors. If the dog is refusing food or water in general and when the owners are present, then this is not a sign of separation anxiety. In such a case, something else is wrong and other considerations should be explored, including potential health issues.

So Is It Really Separation Anxiety?

Dogs with separation anxiety will most likely show more than just one of the above symptoms. Not necessarily at the same time but they will likely show several, if not all of them, at one time or another. They will display these behaviors only when separated, every time they are separated, as soon as they are separated and the behaviors will continue for as long as they are separated. Otherwise, it is probably not separation anxiety.

For example: If the dog is fine for a few hours and then starts misbehaving he is probably just bored. If he only barks at certain times of the day it is probably due to some outside trigger such as mail delivery, the neighbors letting their dog out, school letting out or who knows what that happens at that time. Dogs have excellent hearing so just because you don't hear anything does not mean nothing is happening. If the dog whines and barks for a few minutes and then stops, it is more of a protest than an anxiety issue. He is only filing a complaint right now but may also be letting you know that separation anxiety is in the works. So, prevention is in order.

What's Next?

If you notice patterns like the ones just listed in your dog's behavior, please continue reading, because your dog probably has a case of separation anxiety. If these patterns don't seem to fit or you feel these behaviors are more extreme than your dog is currently demonstrating, he may just be bored or in need of some proper physical and mental exercise. That said, you could also be seeing red flags, indicating the onset of separation anxiety in the making. This book is helpful for prevention as well as treatment of a full blown problem.

CHAPTER 3 – CAUSES: HOW DOGS GET SEPARATION ANXIETY

Before diving into rehabilitation plans, it's a good idea to get a sense of what may have caused the dog to have separation anxiety in the first place. If we know what created the problem, we have a better chance of eliminating it. These things are also good to know if you ever bring home a new dog, so you can avoid creating the problem from the outset.

"An ounce of prevention is worth a pound of cure."
— Benjamin Franklin

Too Much Affection

Affection is great but it really needs to be doled out appropriately. Most of the clients I see give their dogs way too much affection in general and they also give it out for free. By this, I mean the dogs never have to earn it; they can get it anytime they want simply by looking cute. If that doesn't work they can get affection by whining, barking or nudging a person's hand. Am I right? Of course your dog is the cutest one on the planet, so is mine, but being cute is not everything. Even supermodels have to work! People don't just show up to their homes with wheelbarrows full of money. They have to go out on photo shoots, wear constricting outfits and then look cute for the camera - even in uncomfortable weather conditions.

Too much of a good thing can be a bad thing. Besides, your dog has a greater purpose than just looking cute. Dogs need a job and a sense of purpose, just like people do. They can, however, become addicted to having constant attention when you are in their presence to the point where being alone is literally causing them to experience fear and stress.

"If the contrast between your presence and absence is too great you will be on the road to separation anxiety."

Lack of Experience

Sometimes it is not even known that a dog has a separation issue because the dog has never been alone, until one day something in the daily routine changes and the drama begins. This is often the case when the dog lives with a retired person who is always home or a family setting in which at least one family member is always home. It can also be that there are other pets that are always home. Then one day something changes....Mom gets a job, the kids go off to college, the other pet passes on, the retired owner goes to the hospital....you get the picture. Eventually, the dog winds up needing to be left alone and was never prepared for it. This sudden onslaught of solitude can be traumatic for the dog.

Traumatic Experience

In addition to the general lack of experience, or what behaviorists would call lack of conditioning or desensitization that we saw above, is the potential that the dog has had negative experiences with being left alone. This can happen very quickly. If the negative experience is traumatic enough or if it happens during a critical developmental period, one bad experience can be all it takes.

The trauma can be due to loud noises like thunderstorms, but sometimes trauma comes in a well-intended disguise. Puppies tend to go through a period between 8-10 weeks of age called a Fear Imprint Period. During this time puppies are very susceptible to being frightened and experiencing that fear can leave a long-lasting impression or imprint. This also tends to be the time period when most puppies are adopted to a new home. The adoption itself might be frightening for a puppy, as you can imagine, but the situation is usually buffered by loads of love and attention. So the pup makes the move smoothly from the litter to the new home. Happy, happy, happy - everybody's happy and the pup gets played with, stroked and given lavish amounts of toys all weekend long. He even sleeps in bed with the kids. The thought bubble above the puppy's head might look something like, "How wonderful this new place is!" Then Monday comes and doomsday hits. You think you hate Mondays? This little guy has never been alone in his life and now he is stuck in a crate or laundry room or who knows what form of confinement and abandoned for a long period of time. Everyone goes off to school and work and the pup is traumatized during a critical part of his brain development. This can be a bad deal and now he is a good candidate for separation anxiety.

Unhealthy Attachment

Many dogs will be fine as long as there is someone around, even another animal, just as long as they are not completely alone. Others, however, get overly attached to one particular person and are unable to deal with being away from him or her, even with a house full of people. This is often times due to too much affection combined with no practice of being apart from this special person.

Spoiled Dogs

The spoiled dog appears to have never been denied anything. He gets every little thing he wants on a whim but what he has ultimately been denied is the opportunity to develop the coping mechanisms necessary to deal with frustration. He has been denied a sense of independence and strength of character. This leads to the manic behaviors that can be seen when the dog is left alone.

Make no mistake; a spoiled dog is not the same as a fulfilled dog. People tend to think of the word spoiled to mean pampered and loved. It is looked at as being cute as they say, "Oh I know I spoil him, but he's my baby." This may sound cute, but it can actually be very harmful to a dog. The term 'to spoil' actually means to rot or go bad. This is why it is often said that a child is spoiled rotten or a spoiled brat. Separation anxiety is but one of a myriad of behavior issues stemming from dogs being spoiled by well-intended owners. It is important to recognize the dog's bad behavior as a request for fulfillment. The dog will never say, "Hey, I need some structure in my life." They will let you know by acting up, much like an unruly child.

"What does that have to do with separation anxiety?"

Spoiled dogs tend to be overindulged, which leads to what's known as Frustration Intolerance. Have you ever seen a child that has never heard the word no? Have you ever seen one of these children being denied something they want for the first time? It's ugly, right? Well, leaving a spoiled dog behind is pretty much the same. It will be ugly! They will throw a tantrum about being left behind just like a spoiled child being denied what he wants in a toy store. It could be argued that this is not truly separation anxiety but the symptoms and solutions are pretty much the same, so let's just go with it.

"Will the real baby please stand up?"

Consider this: If a human, who has a much more developed intellect and ability to reason than a dog, can actually begin to think of a predatory animal as their own child then how much of a stretch would it be to assume a dog is capable of the same error? No stretch at all in my view, which is why I say "If you treat your dog like a baby, she will think that you are the baby!" This will cause a dog to feel responsible for you which, as you can imagine, will cause anxiety when you leave her alone. This is not a case of the dog acting like a scared child but of the dog acting like a parent who is scared for her child (you). Possible? I think so. Jan Fennell makes this comparison in her book "The Dog Listener" and I think it rings true. What would you do if your three year-old child had somehow locked you in the house and was wandering around outside? Would you panic? Would you scream? Would you try to break out of the house to protect your child? I think you would.

You must be a parent to your dog inasmuch as you are responsible for her well-being and development, but this is much different than thinking your dog is a cute, furry little baby. You should achieve a level of love and friendship with your dog but also a level of status as an authority figure. Cute and furry as she is, she is a dog, a relative of the wolf, a pack animal and she needs a position in her pack. She does not need to be the leader, she needs to know she has a leader and that's you. That's what a doggie parent is, a leader, not a spoiler.

Lack of Leadership

As pack animals, dogs are hardwired with a certain need for leadership. This does not mean that all dogs want to be the "top dog" or "alpha dog," but what it does mean is that they need to feel confident that the role is taken. Many of my clients seem to feel like being their dog's leader is somehow demeaning or unfair to the dog. To the contrary! Having a competent leader is very comforting to a dog.

A general lack of structure and direction can lead a dog to assume the burden of responsibility. Let me emphasize that. I said the burden, not the joy, of responsibility. This burden is stressful and can cause anxiety. It's really no different than throwing an unprepared employee into the role of his manager, expecting that he'll be able to handle the additional workload, even though he has never had this level of responsibility before. Stressful, for sure! Being the boss may have a few perks but it comes at a high price and most dogs, just like most people, are not suited for it.

Lack of Exercise

"A tired dog is a good dog."

This is a well-known canine behavior mantra for good reason. Pent up energy can cause or exaggerate just about any behavior problem under the sun, including separation anxiety. While lack of exercise alone may not create separation anxiety, it will certainly exaggerate the issue. What might be only minutes of mild whining in a regularly-exercised, tired dog will likely become hours of loud barking in a dog that is busting at the seams with excessive energy. At first, this may only be the dog's way of releasing energy and venting frustration, but, if this goes on repeatedly, it can lead to chronic stress which is conditioned through association with being alone, which leads to separation anxiety. It's a lesson in Learning Theory 101. Very interesting, isn't it?

Important Note: By lack of exercise, I mean both mental and physical. Most people fall short on both, but particularly so on the mental aspect. Some dogs are so high energy that the average person will not be able to physically tire them out. Attempts to tire a high energy dog through physical exercise alone will often only build stamina and create an overstimulated-super-athlete that needs more and more exercise and never really settles down. Lack of mental exercise can turn a high-energy dog into a high-strung dog. The difference is that a high-strung dog will tend to be chronically anxious and have a hard time being calm. This dog will likely always be on edge and this can easily play into a separation anxiety issue.

Health Issues

Health conditions such as Hypothyroidism and Vaccinosis can cause symptoms of separation anxiety. If you have an extreme case, an unexplained or sudden onset of this anxious behavior or you find that behavior modification from an expert is not helping, you may need a vet check to ensure there isn't an underlying medical issue.

Spite or Revenge?

I've had many clients who are sure that their dog is behaving maliciously out of spite because he is angry about being left alone and wants to get even with them. This is a human way of thinking, not a canine way of thinking. Dogs can do a lot of damage due to uncontrolled emotions such as stress, frustration, boredom, fear or panic but I don't believe they are capable of being spiteful in the way that humans are.

The destructive dog is not getting even or trying to "teach you a lesson" for leaving, they are just venting or doing things that make them feel better. When I was 17, I broke my hand by punching a solid oak door with all my might. Why? Because I was mad at my girlfriend. I was reacting without thinking and I needed to release my rage. There was no plot to spite her or teach her a lesson, I was just upset and that's it. This is more like a dog, just simple, honest, unadulterated emotional release. So, don't overthink it.

What if I'm wrong about that?

Science is learning new things about the cognitive powers of dogs all the time, so I will remain open to the possibility that I'm wrong, but my research and experience to date confirm my position. Even if it was the case that dogs were capable of being spiteful to get even and teach us a lesson, it would fall under a different category. Separation anxiety is an actual state of fear or panic, not revenge.

Until proven otherwise though, let's assume I'm right. Assumptions to the contrary cause a ton of problems in canine-human communications. If dogs had the same thought process as humans there would be little need for dog trainers or behaviorists.

CHAPTER 4 – SOLUTIONS: HOW TO CURE SEPARATION ANXIETY

If you recognize any of the symptoms from chapter two and/or causes from chapter three, then you may have deduced by now that, outside some unusual medical issue, the problem most likely stems from a human-caused relationship issue as opposed to a defective-dog issue. You may have already deduced from the list of causes that there are some things you need to change, but let's get into the details to ensure success.

Behavior modification for separation anxiety ranges from very simple to very complicated. The level of difficulty depends on how severe and deep-rooted the dog's condition is and the willingness of the owner to go along with the recommended lifestyle changes. The latter, as you may have guessed, is more often than not the bigger hurdle. I typically go to people's homes, evaluate the case and then proceed with recommending a course of action. Most people are not interested in learning all the ins and outs of it, they just want the simplest and fastest solutions possible and I do my best to give them exactly that. However, since this is a book and I am not there to pick and choose only the parts you need to focus on, I have to do my best to cover the full spectrum of possibilities. It is my intention to be thorough and I highly recommend following the whole plan step by step for optimal results.

This chapter is broken down into four sections:

1. When You Are Home
2. Preparing for Departure
3. Making Your Exit
4. Leaving Before Your Dog is Ready

Section 1 - When You Are Home

It may seem counter-intuitive but a majority of separation anxiety problems are actually caused while the humans are home and, therefore, need to be treated while the humans are home. Most people dealing with separation anxiety are unintentionally harming their dog by loving them the wrong way.

"What do you mean I love my dog the wrong way?"

Let me explain. Affection is only one expression of love. There's more to it than that! Truly loving a dog is much deeper than simply enjoying their company and the feel of their fur. To truly love a dog is to provide them with what they really need. That may mean what some people call "tough love" or discipline. As we touched on in the previous chapter, dogs need the fulfillment, a sense of purpose and independence that they are actually deprived of through constant doting or spoiling. Think about it. If you are constantly petting and paying attention to your dog when you are around, then it makes perfect sense that he will have a difficult time dealing with your absence. If I had to put it in one sentence it would be this:

"Downplaying your presence is absolutely the number one way to help a dog deal with your absence."

With that said, there are also a lot of potential details in treating separation anxiety and there are a ton of things that you can and should do with your dog as much as possible. Some are directly related to the specific problem, some are more holistic or foundational, but all are valuable. The treatments outlined in this chapter are beneficial for all dogs, with or without separation anxiety. Most, if not all, of the following suggestions fall into the category of a panacea, cure-all or what I call "Leadership 101."

Here are some tips on how to downplay your presence, increase your leadership, fulfill your dog's true needs and condition your dog to your absence.

This section is divided into two parts:

- Part 1 - Limited Affection and Attention
- Part 2 - Unlimited Activities

Part 1: Limited Attention

"Too much of a good thing? Less is more? What?!"

These conundrums I never understood as a kid. I thought, "How can this be? If a little is good, surely a lot is even better!" Now that I'm a little longer in the tooth, I totally get it. I remember being a young boy, just old enough to make Kool-Aid unsupervised, my friends and I finally learned that, yes, you can indeed add too much sugar. I'm sure you have some stories of your own about how you learned to embrace these concepts, at least in cases that don't involve dogs.....cute, cuddly, sweet, lovable dogs....you can't have too much of that kind of sugar....can you?

As discussed earlier, too much attention, particularly in the form of affection, tends to be the main culprit in creating separation anxiety as well as a host of other behavior problems. I get a ton of resistance on this one, but it should be obvious that if this is the problem then the solution is going to be to stop doing it. Right? It's like that old comedy skit where the guy says, "Hey Doc, it hurts when I do this." Then the doctor says, "Don't do that." The difference here is that I'm not going prescribe never giving your dog any attention; I'm just going to suggest some rules to put around the attention.

"There are a thousand hacking at the branches of evil to one who is striking at the root." - Henry David Thoreau

Although we are not discussing evil, I believe that quote can apply to just about anything. Getting to the root of the problem is certainly the most holistic solution, and also has the best chance of long-term success with the least chance of side effects. Although we live in a quick-fix society, more and more people are turning to holistic or "alternative" medicine when it comes to their health. These modalities focus on the patient as a whole rather than the disease and aim to eliminate the root cause of the problem rather than simply suppress the symptoms with medication. No one can objectively argue the logic of this in regards to physical health and I would say this logic also applies to mental health, including canine mental health. The problem lies not in logic but in compliance. Whether talking to a doctor or a dog trainer, most people will likely have massive amounts of resistance due to the fact that it means making lifestyle changes.

"Do I really have to...."

- Stop eating sugar?
- Drink water rather than soda?
- Go to bed earlier?
- Get more exercise?
- Stop petting my dog so much?

"That's crazy talk! Just give me a pill and let me live my life!"

This is a common response and totally understandable. People are naturally resistant to change but in order to improve your health, your dog's behavior or anything else in your life, you must fight this reflexive response. You must move from resistance to persistence. How can you expect change if you are unwilling to change? Learn to embrace the change and know that it is for the benefit of all involved....you, your dog and probably your neighbors.

So, now that I've set the stage and sold you on the idea, let's look at some strategies for putting limitations on attention and affection. Don't worry, it will only hurt a little.

Play Hard To Get

Most people will recognize the phrase "play hard to get" as a form of dating advice. Generally speaking, it means not to come off as desperate or easy. You know, wait three days before calling, five dates before that first kiss and so on. These are generally accepted ground rules in the world of dating but they are also some of the most broken rules on the planet.

This is because they make sense logically but not emotionally.

Guess what? You don't want to come off as desperate or easy in the eyes of your dog, either! While a "sure thing" may have a certain appeal, it does not demand respect or create loyalty. In other words, you don't want to be taken for granted and/or taken advantage of by your dog.

This is relevant to ALL dog owners, even those without a separation issue, because it provides a foundation for good leadership and makes your value skyrocket. If your dog can get you to pet him or throw the ball for him anytime he wants then why should he listen to you when he is occupied with something novel or interesting? If he could talk he might say, "Yeah, I hear you but can't you see I'm busy? I'll get back to you a little later when I need a belly rub." So don't play the game that way. Play hard to get!

Separation anxiety is almost always a side effect of too much free attention and a lack of quality leadership. You need to go on a strict policy of putting all attention on your terms. Like a special event or some high profile Hollywood party, your attention will be by invitation only. Having your dog value your relationship as a fine dining experience rather than a quick drive-thru at some fast food joint will do a world of good for your relationship with your dog. This will help limit the amount of affection and attention your dog gets from you and will make him appreciate it all the more when he does get it. This, in-turn, will help him to be more relaxed and independent.

Many people, even professional trainers and behaviorists, often miss the nuances of connection and get caught up in suppressing the symptoms. It's like looking for the right type of pain medication but not looking for the cause of the pain. Many people will get caught up in the act of leaving the dog alone, since that's the outward problem, but they fail to look at the overall relationship, which is the underlying cause of the anxiety in the first place.

So, the biggest hurdle is usually not the dog, it's the human. Most dog-lovers, and especially those in separation anxiety cases, just can't stop petting and overindulging their dog. Please, bite the bullet and follow the plan. You'll have won half the battle.

I don't mean to make it sound as if your dog will accept this new program without a fight. Au contraire! He will most likely try harder than ever to get your attention. He may bark, whine, nudge your arm, drop a toy in your lap, jump on you or display any assortment of previously successful behaviors. By previously successful, I mean that they have gotten your attention in the past. Some of that attention may have even been in the form of reprimands or attempted punishment, which can actually wind up being interpreted as a reward by the dog. Often, in the dog's mind, any attention is good attention. Not anymore, though, because you will ignore all demands for attention. That's right; completely ignore the dog as if he is a ghost. Don't look at him, don't pull your arm away as he nudges it and don't walk around him as he blocks your path. Do the walk through, which means walk through rather than around the dog if he gets in your path and certainly don't say, "No" or utter any other words. He is not there, he is a ghost! It's as simple as that. Another way of saying this, made famous by Cesar Millan on the hit TV series Dog Whisperer is "No Touch, No Talk, No Eye Contact." This concept is simple in theory, yet so difficult in practice. Don't worry, you are not alone….

Almost every client that I have ever worked with has failed to get this whole ignore-the-dog-thing right the first time out of the gate. For example: They will say, "OK, I understand…" and then the dog will lick their hand and they will pull it away, look at the dog and say, "No!" Or, the dog will walk in front of them and the human will stop or go around the dog. This is not ignoring the dog. Dogs are acutely aware of every move we make, masters of reading body language and experts at figuring out what works for them and what does not. I have to point it out to my clients because they are unaware of their own actions. "I did?" is what I typically hear when I say "You moved your hand and looked at the dog." Then we have a laugh about it and try again. This is a book so I am not there to help you. It is up to you to pay close attention to your own actions. Don't worry if you mess up, just be aware of it. It is reflexive to pull or move away from a jumping, licking dog and even harder not to look at them so you must train yourself. It will take a little practice but you can do it.

"Why no eye contact?"

I suppose I should make a quick comment on the importance of no eye contact during these exercises. Eye contact is engaging and the whole idea of the exercise is to be non-engaging with the dog. If you doubt the power of eye contact try this little experiment: go to a restaurant, coffee shop or, if you're really brave, a bar and take a seat. Now pick a random person at another table and stare at him or her. That's it, just stare and keep staring.

Do not make any expression… just put on your best poker face. What do you reckon might happen? You may get a phone number or you may get in a fight but you will no doubt get some kind of reaction. You will be affecting that person's experience and invading their space, even though you are across the room. That is the power of eye contact and it is not lost on your dog.

I will be the first to admit that these exercises are easier said than done, but so is pretty much anything in life that is worth working for. It is extremely important, though, so please persevere. The technique of ignoring is technically called extinction, which means the behavior will extinguish on its own through lack of reinforcement. The downside is that it requires patience and is almost certain to bring on an extinction burst, which means it will get worse before it gets better. This is because these behaviors have worked in the past so the dog will think he simply needs to try harder. He may bark louder, jump higher or scratch harder to get your attention. The upside however is that you can avoid the complications of using punishment, which is particularly important pertaining to separation anxiety.

Important note on the use of punishment: In cases when the dog is actually causing pain or injury in his attempts for attention and in cases when clients simply don't have the patience to tolerate an extinction burst, punishment may be required. If a verbal reprimand in a quick firm tone does the trick then that's fine but in most cases that either doesn't work at all or makes matters worse because the dog sees it as attention or a game. In such a case you should hire a professional in your area who understands the proper use punishment. Punishment can be tricky to use effectively and appropriately and is beyond the scope of this book.

Please keep in mind that I am not suggesting that you don't give your dog attention. When it's time for attention you can call him over to you for a belly rub or a toss of the ball. What I'm suggesting is that you always be the one who initiates the attention or activity, not the dog.

Your dog's world should look something like this:

- Whining & Barking   =   No Attention
- Laying Down Quietly =   Belly Rubs
- Pawing & Licking You =   No Attention
- Coming When Called =   Petting & Fetch

That's what is meant by "on your terms" and "by invitation only."

When choosing the right moment to give your dog some attention, be very aware that *What You Pet Is What You Get*. This means that anything you reward will increase in strength and frequency. This includes outward behaviors as well as your dog's mental state. Pay attention to your dog's state of mind. Only initiate interactions when the dog is calm, not anxious. Again, this is a simple concept, right?

Once you master the art of playing hard to get, you will start to notice that your dog no longer......well, actually you will start to notice that you don't notice her. Sounds funny I know, but this is a good thing. You may find yourself for the first time wondering, "Where's Daisy?" Then you notice that she is content on her bed, breathing normally and doesn't need to be coddled or entertained all the time. You may soon find that you can get up to go to the bathroom without Daisy following you! This brings us to the next step.

No Shadowing

As we saw in the Symptoms chapter, most dogs with separation anxiety tend to follow their owners like a shadow. Simple solution... don't allow this to continue. You must break the habit immediately and consistently. There are a few simple ways to do this:

Rule number one is No Hi - No Bye. This means don't make a big fuss when coming and going. Come and go with no fanfare whatsoever, never saying hello or goodbye. The idea that you want to build on is that you come and you go and it's no big deal. This will eventually be built upon as you begin leaving the house, but for now you will just be in the house going about your day.

One thing that's fairly easy is to close the door behind you when you go from room to room. The only potential problem is your dog may scratch at the door. Behaviorally, this can simply be ignored but financially this may be a problem, especially if you have nice doors. Otherwise, he will probably just whine, bark, pace and pant. These behaviors are harmless to your house so just ignore them and go about your business. DO NOT talk to him, sooth him or instruct him in any way. He is still a ghost at this point, just go in the room, do your business and come back out. (Exception: if the dog is barging ahead through the door, you will have to block him.)

As you go from room to room, do The Walk Through, which means to walk through the dog, not around the dog, in a straight line as if he's not even there. Be careful not to injure the dog or yourself, but otherwise just walk. If he gets bumped by your legs, that's fine. You are not kicking the dog but you are not yielding your space either. He will learn to respect your personal space and move out of the way soon enough. This is one of those times when you will find that doing nothing is harder than it sounds but that's basically what you are doing, nothing, just going about your business. (We touched on this previously in the Play Hard To Get Section)

Safety Tips: Don't step on or injure your dog, but do your best to just walk as you would if there was no dog. Use caution and seek professional help if you are dealing with an aggressive dog that may bite you for bumping into him or invading his space.

Another fairly easy shadowing solution is to use a tether or tie-out. All you really need in most cases is a leash and a heavy or solid object to tie it to. Tie the leash to a table leg, banister or anything that is strong enough to hold the dog without being broken or pulled over. Now the dog cannot shadow you as you go about your business. I would recommend having the dog tethered near you, maybe even right next to you, as you read, watch TV or whatever you are into. Simply ignore the dog and go about your business. When you get up to go to the bathroom or get a drink he will be unable to follow you. DO NOT talk to him or even look at him for that matter. Just get up, do your thing and sit back down. That's it. Your dog may go nuts or may just whimper a bit, this is a barometer of how bad of a case of separation anxiety you are dealing with. Regardless, your job is to do nothing. That's it, just do nothing. Sounds easy but it's not, so remember, there is no dog right now. You do not hear him or see him, he is a ghost. Some dogs may chew the leash. DO NOT let this get your attention. Don't try to correct him for this because that is just letting him know he is getting your attention. In such a case, you can try a chewing deterrent spray but you will likely need a chain or cable tie-out that is non-destructible. Some people also opt for an eye bolt into the baseboard for a tie-out location, usually for a convenient location or just because they don't have any heavy furniture to tie the dog to.

WARNING: DO NOT tether with a choke chain or slip lead of any sort and NEVER to something from which a dog can hang himself. NEVER leave a tethered dog unsupervised. For example: a dog tethered to a couch leg can jump over the back of the couch and hang herself. This can be very dangerous so use caution and common sense. The safest way is to tether the dog to a harness rather than a collar.

Baby gates are another anti-shadowing option, much like closing doors behind you, but these can create a bit more distance between you and the dog by keeping him out of entire sections of the house. For example: as you go from the kitchen to the bathroom and then down the hall to the bedroom he will have to watch from the family room. This gives the dog a bit more freedom than the tether. Some dogs can and will jump over the gate, but most of the time they work very well.

Crates and Ex-Pens (exercise pens) are also anti-shadowing options. Ex-pens offer a little more room for movement than crates and require less desensitization and counter-conditioning (conditioning that is intended to replace a negative responsive to a stimulus with a positive response), but some dogs can jump over them, knock them down and/or injure themselves attempting to escape.

Crate Training is a topic unto itself. I would not use a crate in the beginning stages of treating separation anxiety unless the dog has already been conditioned to the crate. Crating can be stressful enough even when dogs do not have a separation issue because it feels like a trap. On the other hand, many dogs love their crate and feel safe inside it like a den. This requires proper conditioning and may take days or weeks to accomplish. Conditioning a dog to enjoy the crate can come in very handy but if the dog already has separation anxiety I would start with all the previous options and add the crate a little later. Otherwise, the dog will be conditioned to hate the crate, which will be a huge setback.

No Dogs On The Furniture

Many dog-lovers really enjoy having their dogs on the furniture with them. Many seem to feel as though that's the only reason for having dog! I hate to take this joy away from my clients and in most cases I do not. Separation anxiety, however is one of those cases when I must insist on keeping the dog off the furniture. Yes, that includes the bed as well as the couch. Why? Because we must stick with the theme that I believe I have made clear at this point, which is to create some distance and downplay your presence. The difference between being on the floor and being in your lap may only be a few feet, but it is still creating a minor separation and that is exactly what we need to do to desensitize the dog. This little mole hill is actually a mountain! It will automatically help you stick with the program and avoid giving too much affection. If the rule is that you have to get on the floor in order to pet or cuddle with your dog, how often will you do it and for how long? Chances are it will be a lot less than if the dog is up on the couch with you because it's uncomfortable and you have to go out of your way to do it. So please, bite the bullet and keep the dog on the floor where you can put a nice comfy dog bed. Don't worry; this may not have to be forever.

Once everything is totally stabilized and you have no signs of separation anxiety whatsoever, you can try adding some furniture time back into the mix. Most clients actually find that they don't mind having the dog stay on the floor and just keep things that way, others will add it back in successfully and others will find it causes a setback and start seeing the old symptoms come back. Every case is different, but I generally recommend just sticking with the no furniture policy as it's the most fail safe method.

Using the Backyard or Car

Most dogs with separation anxiety will have a problem being alone no matter what, but others are somewhat okay with being alone in the yard or in the car, at least for a little while. They may not be totally relaxed but they don't go totally nuts either. If this is your dog, consider yourself lucky! If you play your cards right, you can use this to begin gradually desensitizing your dog to longer periods of being alone. In these cases, the dog has only developed an anxiety issue in the house, so you want to be careful not to create the same issue with the yard or car by leaving him there for too long. What you want to do is give multiple short spurts of alone time in the car or yard. Remember everything you've learned so far and be sure to come and go with no fanfare whatsoever. Don't say Hi and don't say Bye, just go about your business. This should be fairly easy, so the trick is to do this often and gradually make the alone time longer. The key word there is *gradually*.

Part 2: Unlimited Activities

"Unlimited! Alright! I like the sound of that!"

By now you may be thinking "Well, what the hell do I have a dog for if I have to ignore him all the time?" I now bring you all the joys and activities that you can and should do with a dog that has separation anxiety. Feast to your heart's content on all of the activities below, with the only exceptions to the "unlimited" rule being your dog's fitness, tolerance and interest.

Exercise, Exercise, Exercise

"Fulfilling a dog's exercise needs on a daily basis is critical, not only for the mental and physical health of the dog, but also for the sanity of the owner."

Dogs with separation anxiety should be exercised to the point of exhaustion on a daily basis. Use common sense here, don't run your dog into a heat stroke or anything like that, just get him good and tired. Get that big-old-silly-looking tongue hanging out so that when you stop he just plops down on the ground tired and content. Look at that big ol' slobbery grin. That is happiness, my friend. Good job! An exhausted dog will more likely achieve relaxation, which is the opposite of anxiety. I know, getting your dog good and tired on a daily basis may require spending time and effort that you are not used to but the dividends are well worth the investment. Accomplishing this consistently has a cumulative effect, eventually helping to create a dog that is generally in a relaxed mental state....even when not exhausted.

Every dog is different, so it's important to note that fulfilling the dog's needs means meeting the requirements of that individual dog. That is to say, providing what actually is enough, not what you think should be enough. A daily 30 minute walk will be enough for some dogs, while others will need to jog or run alongside a bicycle for two hours, plus play fetch for 30 minutes and that will take care of just the morning. By the afternoon, they will be chomping at the bit and ready for more action.

In the book "The 7 Habits of Highly Effective People" by Stephen R. Covey, the fourth habit is "Think Win-Win." Going for a daily walk is the ultimate win-win and should be the cornerstone of every dog's life. Walking is the key to living a long, healthy, happy life and that means for humans and canines alike. Plus you and your dog can do it together! That's a win-win situation for sure! Having a dog is like having a walking partner and your own personal motivational fitness coach! They will remind you and inspire you to get up off your butt and go for a walk when you might have otherwise just kept on watching reruns of your favorite sitcom. "Ugh!" You might say at first, but you will feel better once you get up and do it, I promise.

Going for a walk is great low impact exercise and, in my view, one of the best ways to bond with a dog. It's also a great way to get fresh air and free vitamin D. Did you know that? Sunlight has vitamin D-boosting benefits! Walking and vitamin D are also both important for heart health. The social benefits are massive, as well. It's amazing how many people get to know their neighbors by walking their dogs. This is awesome for the humans but the benefits to the dog are even greater. Dogs need to get out in the world and experience all the different sights, sounds, and smells in order to be mentally sound and happy. A mentally sound and fulfilled dog will be much less likely to have anxiety issues.

A major foundational mantra chanted by behaviorists everywhere is "Dogs need to be socialized!" It is one of the few things that all behaviorists agree on without exception and it happens naturally, to one degree or another, simply by going for a walk. See, that's a win-win to say the least, probably more like a win-win-win!

Mental Exercise

As mentioned earlier in the Causes Chapter, exercise is not just physical, dogs also need mental exercise. Mental exercise will drain energy as well as develop mental discipline. Those with mentally demanding jobs can attest to this because they come home tired from a hard day's work just as much as those whose work entails primarily physical labor. This is true for dogs, as well. Some high energy dogs are nearly impossible to tire physically and attempts to do so will only build their stamina, requiring more and more exercise. Physical exercise alone may get them tired temporarily, but can also be mentally over stimulating, creating an unstable, unbalanced mind. These dogs may never actually achieve calmness other than when totally exhausted. This is not truly a dog with a calm mental state; it is just an illusion which won't last long. In reality, they are just re-charging their battery.

All dogs, especially high energy dogs, need to be taught what I call The Art of Doing Nothing, which translates to doing non-active exercises. An example would be putting your dog in a Down-Stay position and having him hold that position for a long period of time around major distractions. Imagine reading at a coffee shop with Rover relaxed by your feet.

High energy dogs also need to have plenty of impulse control and mental challenges built into their daily exercise. An example would be walking in a strict Heel position with no sniffing, pulling or lunging. Walking at a human pace is really not much exercise for a dog physically but a structured "obedience" walk requires a ton of mental discipline, which is added exercise, which is very valuable for our goal of calmness. You see, a dog that is pacing to and fro on the walk, going ahead, behind, left, right and so forth may be getting in a few extra steps along the way, but a dog that is expected to walk at your side will be much more stable-minded, well-behaved, disciplined and, most important of all, relaxed. Relaxation is, of course, the opposite of anxiety.

It is important to drain the dog's energy on a daily basis and in ways that are not constantly over stimulating. Remember, we are talking about separation anxiety and the opposite of anxiety is calmness. The impulse control gained through mental exercise, plus the energy drained by physical exertion is the perfect equation for a calm dog. The benefits of this potent combination are cumulative, so it needs to be done on a daily basis to be effective. It's similar to working out at the gym. You can't be lazy all week and then pump iron all day on Saturday. Well, you can, but you will only make yourself sore and possibly sustain an injury.

You can only achieve and maintain fitness by exercising on a regular basis and a good starting point is the simple, structured daily walk.

Training Games

I am putting training games under the "UN-limited" umbrella, but there is a caveat: these activities must be totally under your control. That is why I'm calling them training games rather than simply "games." The by-invitation-only rule still applies, so you will say when the game starts, when it stops and control all the rules in between.

Teaching your dog to play a proper game of Fetch or Tug can be great fun and great exercise. The key word there is *proper*, which means you must train and maintain control of the game. Done properly, these games are physically and mentally challenging for the dog and require quite a bit of discipline. The dog should return the toy to you immediately and release it on command. He should not try to take it from your hand; he must wait until given his cue to chase the ball or bite the tug toy. Tug should never be a power struggle between you and the dog; it should be a shared event. Even if the dog "wins" he should come right back for more play rather than run off to hoard his "prize."

It is also great to include some obedience exercises into the games, making the dog do a Sit before being released to chase the ball or do a Down in the middle of a game of Tug for example.

I see a lot of clients with dogs that are what I call "Ball Crazy." Enthusiasm for the ball is fine; it's the "Crazy" part that is not healthy. These dogs will run themselves sick as long as someone is willing to keep throwing the ball or Frisbee or whatever. If there is a ball around they care about nothing else. If there is not a ball around they will look for one or maybe find a stick to continuously drop at your feet. Sometimes they will just follow you around looking at you as if to say "Come on, where are you hiding it? I know you have it, now stop messing around and throw it!" Owners of these dogs tend to think it's cute or funny but, unfortunately, this can be a neurotic or compulsive behavior. A normal, healthy dog, given a chance, will want to explore the environment by sniffing. A dog that is off-leash at the beach and does nothing but look at you or bark at you to throw the ball, even when you don't have a ball, is in an unnatural, unhealthy, unbalanced state.

Let me clarify. There is nothing wrong with a dog having a strong play drive and a love of the game. That's fantastic! The point I'm trying to make is that it should not be an obsession. You need to give your dog an on-off switch. This means that when you whip out the ball it's game on and when you put it away it's game off, simple as that. If you are at an off-leash dog beach and your dog will play fetch with you around all those distractions you are in good shape, you have engagement, that's awesome! On the other hand, if you don't have a ball or you put it in your pocket and the dog won't stop begging for more, you have some kind of mental instability going on. This may or may not be connected to separation anxiety, but it needs to be dealt with because, chances are, it probably does. One form of anxiety can lend itself to another and all forms of anxiety are stressful. Besides, these dogs are missing out on a wonderful opportunity to just run around and be a dog.

Training games are also a good time to use the backyard if you have one or go outside in some way. Too much excitement in the house is probably not a good idea for any dog and especially for a dog with separation anxiety. Remember, the name of the game is calmness. We want the dog to associate being indoors with being calm. Some indoor play is okay but I would try to take the exciting stuff outside and especially the backyard, since it will help create a positive association with being out there.

Obedience Training

Obedience Training is highly valuable to any human-dog relationship. It helps the dog see you as an authority figure, establishes a clear cross-species communication system and provides a healthy sense of your leadership. I would recommend at least learning the five basic commands of Sit, Down, Stay, Come and Heel. The one of particular importance to dogs with separation anxiety is Stay. It is a great command to teach your dog because it gives you the opportunity to distance yourself from your dog (whether it's 6 feet away or around the corner) and he'll learn that you will always come back. Advancing your Stays to the point of being able to go out of sight is key not only for obedience but also for trust. You can also teach your dog to "Go To Bed" which is basically just a Down-Stay but with a send-off to a comfy location.

Scent Games and Tricks

"A dog would just as soon pee on a Rembrandt as look at it."

He would, of course, smell it first; it would be disrespectful not to! So what if you saw a person sniffing every piece in an art gallery? Would you find that strange? Of course you would! It would be obviously weird and would stand out to you in a second. That's the way I feel when I see a dog, ball-crazy or otherwise, that doesn't use his nose. Whenever I am working with a client and notice that their dog is not using his nose to sniff me or to check out a new environment, I know something is off. Whether they are staring at me out of fear or staring at me because they want to bite, they are using their eyes rather than their nose to check me out and that's a red flag.

Search-and-Scent games are great fun for many dogs, but more importantly, they get the dog working at a distance from you and help build some independence. Start by tossing a treat on the floor where they can see it, then toss it so it goes behind a chair or around a corner and then start to hide it and encourage the dog to "go find" or whatever cue you prefer. Start simple, maybe leaving a trail of small treats leading to a big one, and then make the games harder and harder. If you have a backyard, then play these games out there, as well. At first, play these games while you supervise, but the goal is to work up to leaving the room while the dog searches unsupervised -

first in the house and then in the backyard. This builds independence and creates a positive association with being alone, both indoors and outside.

Tricks also fall under the unlimited category. Teaching your dog to rollover, high-five, spin in circles or any other fun tricks is just that: fun. It won't really have an effect on separation anxiety one way or another, but it is great mental exercise for your dog, so feel free to go for it. Friends and family will love to see you put on a doggy circus when they visit and who knows? Maybe you'll even become a star on the internet!

Use the Backyard or Outdoors

Now that we've introduced the backyard for games and such, we can also use it for all that affection you are bound to be missing. Remember, we are still in the limited attention stage while in the house, but when you just can't stand it and need to give your dog some affection, all you have to do is go outside. If you are lucky enough to have a backyard, then use it. This is a place you can go for UN-limited attention and activities. Play games, do some obedience training or just hang out and give your dog some love. Have your coffee or eat lunch out there while your dog chews on a bone or stuffed Kong toy.

The backyard has potential as a future place for your dog to spend some alone time, so this is a great way to give it a positive association. Your dog should view the backyard as a happy place, not a place of banishment. I see way too many clients that put the dog outside as punishment for bad behavior. I also see many clients with backyards that still keep their dogs in the house all the time. What a waste! The backyard is often an untapped gold mine! Think about it. Dogs are meant to be outside, not locked up in a house all day, plus they can go to the bathroom whenever they want rather than having to hold it all day. Some dogs can do alright in the house all the time, but most will go a little crazy. Sure, they love to be in the house, but not trapped in the house 24/7. They were born to be outside. I would go crazy in the house all the time and I'm not even a dog!

"What about barking and destruction?"

Barking and destructive behaviors can deter people from leaving their dog outside, but these things can be resolved and are well worth the effort. Remember, at this point we are only spending time out there with the dog, not leaving her alone. As we cure the separation anxiety, the barking and destructive behaviors will go away. There is, of course, the potential for other forms of barking, such as territorial barking, but those can be dealt with easily compared to separation anxiety. The leadership principles that are intertwined in all the lessons laid out in this book will help minimize the dog's need to behave territorially. Remember, this is a holistic approach and the ripple effects are far-reaching. (I'll discuss more on barking in a minute.)

Leadership

"The kind of leadership that inspires follower-ship comes only when we put service above self." - from The 8th Habit by Stephen R. Covey

As mentioned in the Causes chapter, a lack of leadership can lead to a host of behavioral problems, including separation anxiety, but what does that mean? Terms like leadership, alpha dog, pack leader and the like get hurled around all the time, but they are a bit vague, aren't they? Words themselves tend to be a problem and all you have to do is a brief search on the internet to find all sorts of bantering over semantics. Fortunately, dogs don't understand words, at least not like we do, so let's not get our knickers in a twist over terminology. Can we agree on this? OK, then.

In my view, a good leader is one that is confident, carries authority, commands respect but, more than anything else, a good leader cares first and foremost for the well-being of his followers. A leader may need to give orders or instructions and he may need to enforce the completion of those directives, but he does so gracefully, respectfully and is mindful of the well-being of all involved. He is tough when necessary, but also gentle when that is the need. He is fair and generous, but not careless and not a pushover. He is trusted because he is trustworthy and his policies are always consistent.

I was originally going to devote an entire chapter to leadership, but it turns out that a really great leadership plan is already interwoven into the text of this book. You don't have to be some kind of drill sergeant in order to be your dog's leader, you merely have to set and enforce rules. You need to get and keep your dog in a follower state of mind.

One of the biggest steps towards being a leader in the eyes of your dog is to implement a Nothing in Life is Free or Learn to Earn policy and do so consistently. That means all day, every day, no weekends off.

A lot of what we've talked about up to this point has already established some of this concept, but think about anything and everything of value to your dog that you just might still be giving away for free. How about food? Do you make your dog sit and wait for permission or do you just put the bowl down?

What about going through doors? Do you make your dog wait for permission or does he barge right on through? What about the car door? What about greeting guests or strangers? Do you make your dog sit politely and be calm before getting some attention from them? What about going for a walk? Does your dog sit and wait quietly to get the leash on? Do you control the walk or do you allow the dog to pull?

On and on it goes. There are endless things that happen on a daily basis that you can teach your dog he has to earn. Even if it just means to sit or lay down or come to you, your dog is learning that things don't come for free and that you are the leader and provider whose instructions must be followed. It just may take a little getting used to, but your dog will thank you in the long run. Dogs like to have a sense of structure and they like to work. They feel more secure and confident when they have a leader. It actually takes a load of stress off their shoulders. If your dog sees you as the leader then he won't feel worried about your comings and goings so much. See how that works?

Chew Toy Addiction

Normally, addiction is considered a bad thing, but in his book "Before and After Getting Your Puppy" Ian Dunbar used the term "chewtoyaholic," which I thought was kind of funny when I read it and liked the concept of chew toy addiction. You need to get your dog hooked on long lasting chews of some sort. Stuffed Kongs are a popular choice but some people use raw beef knuckle bones or a variety of other options. The key is to get the dog so fired up on these things, addicted if you will, that nothing else matters. This will be what is used for counter-conditioning in the isolation area. Start by finding out what works for your dog, as they all have different preferences. Then start letting the dog chew on this when tethered or in the ex-pen while you are around, but not interacting with her. She should start to get into it and stop worrying about your business as you go about the house. Come back and sit in the room with her for a while then get up and walk around the house a bit, then come back and sit down again. Rinse and repeat. Simple!

Practice Isolation While You Are Home

So far in this program you have been introduced to the idea of small amounts of separation and how you should and should not interact with your dog when you are home. At this point, it is assumed that you have been playing hard to get, not allowing the dog on the furniture or to shadow you, using a tether and so forth. Are those things going smoothly? Great! If not, continue practicing before moving on to the next step.

Now it's time to create an isolation area that the dog will stay in (and enjoy) when you are not home. This will require some conditioning but should be fairly easy at this point, assuming you've been following all previous instructions.

Step number one is to choose an isolation area that makes the most sense for you. For now this will be short term isolation but you also need to think long term. This should be a safe area where the dog cannot escape, hurt themselves or cause damage to anything valuable. And the more sound proof the better, for your neighbor's sake.

Pre-load the isolation area with that special long lasting chew toy that you have already gotten him hooked on. (See Chew Toy Addiction.) Pre-loading is the key! This means don't let the dog see you put the treat in the isolation area because seeing you prep the area can actually trigger the onset of anxiety. The special treat should be there waiting for him when he goes into his isolation area and over time will create a positive association with being alone in this place. Your dog will now only get this special treat when alone in this dedicated area and no longer in your presence. This is counter-conditioning the dog to look forward to some alone time in this place that magically creates delicious things to chew on. You see, the treat is coming from the area, not from you. It's kind of a reverse psychology thing. Tricky, huh?

Enter and exit the isolation area calmly! No big deal going in, no big deal coming out.

When having your dog enter or exit the isolation area, practice your "Wait" command. He may not be eager to go in at first but eventually he will be chomping at the bit to get in there and see what the treat fairy brought, so at that point, start to practice making him "Wait" for permission. Coming out of the area will likely be the more dramatic moment and the waiting will be more difficult but it's very important. Just remember to be calm and quiet while you do this.

Consistently making your dog wait is not only practical for safety issues and creating calmness, it's also just good leadership. The wait command should be done at all doors...front door, back door, sliding glass door, car door, any and every door, gate or threshold that you can think. It should be made clear to your dog that each of these thresholds are a boundary that require permission to pass.

Never release your dog from his isolation area if he is whining, scratching, barking, panting or being anything other than calm.

Check yourself, as well. Are you calm? Both you and the dog must be calm and quiet. Remember the No Hi, No Bye rule? It still applies. Once released from his isolation area, he will probably charge up again so ignore him for another minute or so until he's calm again to minimize the fanfare. This should all be sinking in by now, but when I'm with clients they usually still need to be reminded. Are you making eye contact? Don't do that, please. (We discussed this earlier under Play Hard To Get.)

If the super-special-isolation-area-treats have not been eaten, then put them away or keep the isolation area closed with the goodies inside. Again, these treats are not to be had in your presence. If this continues to be the case you will need to only feed your dog in the isolation area. This can be while you are home but in a different room.

I am assuming at this point you have already laid the chew toy groundwork discussed earlier. If not, please go back and read Chew Toy Addiction.

Start with short durations and build your way up to longer durations. If the isolation area is a crate, use caution - in extreme cases, dogs will injure themselves trying to escape the crate.

If the isolation area is going to be the backyard, you will want to inform your neighbors of what you are doing. This is because there is a good chance that there will be some barking. (See Using the Backyard, above.)

What About the Barking?

Again, it is important that you not commit to the isolation area until you've already dealt with the shadowing and affection issues in the earlier sections. Once the dog is in the isolation area or backyard, you are committed to wait for calm and quiet behavior. If you reward the barking by giving in, you are doomed.

There will most likely be an "Extinction Burst," which means the unwanted behavior will get worse before it gets better. This is due to the fact that the incessant barking has worked to get attention in the past so, in the dog's mind, the barking must not be loud enough. Be patient and the dog will learn that silence earns your attention and barking is futile.

As a last resort, if the dog is in the backyard barking at the door and you just can't stand it or the neighbors are complaining, you can call her from another door or go around to the gate and call. This is a last resort, don't let miss smarty pants make a connection between her barking and your going to the other door.

This is why I mentioned earlier that the initial isolation area would best be somewhere a little sound proof. The backyard can be a great place to leave your dog, weather permitting of course, but it all depends on the dog. Some dogs actually do better in the backyard, but if you have a barker, it may be hard for the neighbors to go along with the program.

What About Punishment?

Punishment is a very controversial and powerful part of dog training, in general and especially in the case of separation anxiety. All trainers and behaviorists will agree that punishment is sometimes a necessary part of dog training. What they cannot come together on is where to draw the line as to what form of punishment is acceptable and what is not.

As a general rule, punishment is a bad idea with separation anxiety because the dog's condition is an actual state of fear of panic. The dog is not choosing this behavior. With that in mind, it should not be surprising that punishing a dog in this state can potentially cause more anxiety. Bear in mind, barking and destruction are not the problem, they are the symptoms of a problem.

With that said I am a realist and realize some mild corrections may be necessary and even beneficial, risky as they may be. Sometimes a mild correction like a stern "Quiet!" command or a loud bang on the door can be effective in stopping the barking or whining, which will give owners some peace of mind and potentially speed up the whole process.

Please, keep in mind that I am not opening the floodgates for manhandling the dog or anything abusive. I'm talking about maybe using mild corrections.

Whether or not a mild correction or firm corrective command will help or hurt depends heavily on the level and type of training the dog has historically been exposed to. Has the dog been taught a "Quiet" command? Has the dog been trained with corrections or only with positive reinforcement? If the dog has never been corrected or trained in a firm way in the past than an anxiety episode is definitely NOT the time to start.

Any type of corrective or "negative" training should be done at a different time and in a balanced way. Negative commands are those that tell a dog to stop doing something. Commands such as "No" or "Quiet" should be taught in advance and in a scenario that is not part of a separation anxiety meltdown. Physical training should be layered into the basic obedience program and balanced with tons of praise and rewards so that the dog understands it as a basic communication system, not something scary or traumatic. An example would be a mild leash pop to get the dog's attention, which is then followed immediately by praise and a treat. This is all part of a balanced training approach, but beyond the scope of this book. If you and your dog are not already versed in this type of training, then definitely do not try to use any form of punishment to mitigate your dog's separation anxiety.

Disclaimer Alert: Some positive reinforcement purists out there may be upset with me as they read this, but let me put this in perspective. I am a huge advocate for using rewards in training, but "positive" can actually be a "negative" when it fails to get the job done. I have had many clients on the verge of getting rid of a dog who wouldn't stop barking, whining, counter surfing, leash lunging and you-name-it because all the books and TV shows they were reading and watching were strictly based on positive reinforcement. This sounds great to any dog-lover but in reality it wasn't working. Their nerves were frazzled and, in many cases, they were ready to give up on the dog. You know how sometimes it is said that going to a friend's house full of unruly children is a great form of birth control? Well, some of these houses I go to would be a great way to convince a person never to get a dog! Luckily, I know how to raise a dog, so I can see the light through the madness. I show these clients some simple things like how to pop the leash or stand up, give a loud hand clap and firmly say "No!" Simple as that, they have a new dog that they can live with and Rufus doesn't have to go back to the shelter. Yeah! Done properly, these basic corrections are totally harmless and in many cases have literally saved a dog's life. "Oh my God, it's like a miracle" they say and then ask "Why do all these books say I should never do that?" I can only speak for myself and I simply say that there is a time and place for punishment and that it must be handled fairly and properly.

With all that said, I still stand by what I stated earlier, which is that punishment is generally a bad idea when dealing with separation anxiety. Separation anxiety is a special issue so we must use caution. In a nutshell, if a quick corrective command works to quiet the dog, then it's okay to use it. But pay close attention to the effects, as it can easily cause more anxiety, fear or even be interpreted by the dog as a reward by getting your attention, all of which will make things worse.

Look For Triggers

Triggers are things that send a signal to the dog that you are getting ready to leave. These could be putting on your shoes, grabbing your purse or any number of things which can trigger the onset of anxiety. Your dog might hear your keys jiggle, for example, and notice that every time he hears that sound, you leave. Desensitizing your dog to these triggers can help you to get out the door more easily. Once you've identified them, try to disassociate the trigger with you leaving. For example, walk around the house jiggling your keys but don't actually leave. Watch for things that may be much more subtle as well, such as shutting off appliances, topping off your coffee mug or micro subtleties such as your own anxiety. Dogs are like great poker players, they can pick up on microscopic details that make them appear to be psychic, so pay close attention. Sure, it may be a sixth sense, but most likely you are giving away your hand somehow.

Have Your Dog Bond With Other People

As mentioned in the Causes chapter, some dogs will have separation anxiety due to being alone and others only as the result of one particular person's absence. If you notice that the dog is particularly close with one member of the family and shows the most discomfort when this member is gone, have different friends or family members walk, feed, and pet the dog. Hire a dog walker once a week or have a friend come over and take the dog for a trip to the park. At the very least, have different members of the family engage with the dog. All the while, the person with whom the dog has an over attachment issue will be playing hard to get.

Section 2 - Preparing for Departure

Congratulations! I am assuming you didn't cheat and skip ahead to this part...you didn't, did you? Okay, good; that means most of the work is already done and this part is going to be a short read and a piece of cake. Now that you have changed the relationship with your dog through increased structure and less affection you should be seeing some changes. The dog should be feeling less needy, more independent and beginning to see you as a leader rather than a coddler. After all, if you are the leader, it makes more sense for you to come and go as you please, right? So, now it's time to set the stage for actually leaving the house. Here's your to-do list:

Be Calm and Act Normal. This exercise is really no different than what you have already been doing, so just relax. Dogs can sense if you are anxious. The only difference is that you will actually be leaving the house, but we are counting on the fact that the dog probably won't even notice. Seriously, what's the difference if you are at the other end of the house or out of the house? Not much, right? Don't forget to breathe; this should be easy by now.

Pre-Load Your Isolation Area. This is the first thing you need to do because it could be a possible anxiety trigger if done too close to departure. Your dog should already be conditioned to time in this area while you are at home going about your business, with her favorite toy or bone that she doesn't get when you are together. She is, right? Good. Now throw a few easy-to-get treats in there, just some little bits of meat or cheese or something like that, to get her primed. Maybe make a little trail of these leading to your dog's favorite-extra-super-special-long-lasting-treat. Remember, don't let your dog see you do this. It should seem that they appear by magic, making the association with the location and not with you.

Wait, don't put her in there yet, we are only pre-loading right now.

Exercise, Exercise, Exercise! Go for a walk, jog, play fetch...do whatever it takes to get that dog good and tired. A tired dog will be less reactive, less destructive and more prepared to relax. Please do not skip this step and do not underestimate your dog's energy level. Remember, it's not how much you think should make her tired, it's how much actually does.

Avoid Triggers. Even though you have already desensitized your dog to any and all triggers, avoid them for now to increase your chances of a successful departure. Remember, just act normal like you have been doing around the house already.

Leave the TV or Music On. If you typically have these sounds in the house when you are home then leave them on. This keeps things "normal" for the dog. If your house is normally quiet, then skip this.

Are you thinking this all seems a bit redundant? Good! You are spot on. As I said, most of the hard work has already been done in the previous section and all we are doing is getting ready for what should be a smooth exit.

Section 3 - Making Your Exit

Ok, now it's time to put this whole thing to the test. If you have been following all the previous instructions this should be easy. Leaving the house is nothing more than a logical extension of the groundwork which has already been laid. Remember, downplaying your comings and goings is key.

Here are a few tips to make sure it goes smoothly:

Put your tired dog in the pre-loaded isolation area. Do this calmly. No "good-bye" no, "I'll miss you"...no fanfare, nothing different than what you have already been doing. The only difference is that you are actually going to leave the house but the dog doesn't know this, or at least he shouldn't. He will only know something is different if you act differently. Although I do sometimes feel that dogs have a sixth sense of some sort, this is usually due to our subtle actions and biochemistry. If you are stressing out about this your breathing may change or you may even put off a different scent which can be a trigger to the dog that something's up. Be calm, relaxed and "normal" this should be a very easy exercise at this point, assuming you've done your homework.

Leave the House.

Return after 1 minute

No "Hi, I missed you, smoochy...." Just come in and ignore the dog who is still in his isolation area. Go about some household business, watch TV or whatever you normally do. Nothing different than what you have already done other than actually leaving the house.

Repeat a few exits and entrances. Be sure that you are quiet when you are outside the house so the dog really thinks you have left. Assuming things are going well, start gradually extending the time you stay out of the house but be sure to end the exercise before the dog has finished his extra-super-special treat. Remember the idea is to use reverse psychology so that the dog winds up looking forward to a little alone time with his treat. He should be looking at you like "Hey man what's up? No, I'm good here with my treat, I'll be out in a minute." At which point you will take the treat away and he can look forward to finishing it the next time.

Release the dog from the isolation area or yard once he is calm and quiet. Be sure to be calm and quiet yourself. Don't forget to practice the "Wait" exercise. If the isolation area is the backyard just go out and wander around the yard for a few minutes until the dog is calm and away from you. If bringing him inside, practice the "Wait" exercise at the door.

DO NOT say Hi yet. Ignore for a few more minutes until the dog is calm.

Once your dog is calm, then call her to you for a brief, calm greeting. Yes, I said brief. That means a few seconds and calm also means quiet. Don't throw a party. Remember the idea is that this whole ordeal is "no big deal."

Start over from the top randomly throughout the day and gradually increase the duration of departures.

Assuming things are going smoothly, the next step is to start the car and drive away. Some dogs will be fine up until this point because they have associated the car with your long term absence. You may start to hear some whining or barking when you start the car so make it a quick drive around the block and come right back. If the dog really goes nuts at the sound of the car, you can just go outside, start the car, turn it off and come back inside every now and then to break the association.

There you go. That's it. We are done! As you can see, most of the work has to do with your behavior and interactions while you are home with your dog. Once you get those things in order, leaving is really no big deal.

Section 4 - Leaving Before Your Dog is Ready

I know, I know, I hear you screaming, "I have a job! I need to leave RIGHT NOW!" Dealing with time constraints is definitely a problem that most people will have to deal with. I totally get it. This truly is a problem, so let me give a few suggestions on the issue of "right now."

Pet Sitter

Hiring a pet sitter or asking a favor of a friend can be a great option. Be sure to have these people follow the program verbatim. Most pet sitters are dog-lovers but not dog behaviorists, so, you will need to lay down the law with them. They are getting paid to hang out at your house and watch TV, not to cuddle with the dog. If they are qualified, you can also have them walk the dog, but that's about it. The dog is being prepped for being left alone all day, not to have a pet sitter for the rest of his life, so you must be clear on this. The program needs to be followed but it doesn't necessarily need to be you that is doing it. Your dog still may protest that YOU are the one leaving but at least there will be someone there to monitor and follow the plan to make sure your dog doesn't get into too much trouble. It will also provide another person for your dog to bond with.

Doggie Daycare or Boarding Kennel

Doggie daycare is another great option for dogs that like to be around other dogs. They'll get supervised playtime throughout the day, which is fun and energy-burning. Not only do you get the peace of mind that your house is not being destroyed, you get a tired dog at the end of the day. If your dog is antisocial or aggressive towards other dogs, this may not be an option. Some doggie daycares have kennels or separate dog runs for antisocial dogs and may even have a trainer to help with socialization training. Otherwise, a boarding kennel may a good option.

Take the Dog with You

This may not be possible, but many workplaces are dog-friendly as long as your dog is friendly. If you're just running errands around town, many dogs will also show less or no anxiety while waiting in the car assuming it's not a hot day and that you won't be way from the car for too long. I recommend not overcommitting until you see how your dog reacts to being in the car alone. Try a short trip to the gas station before a long lunch with friends.

In a perfect world, you would be able to spend at least a few days working on this program before going back to work, but I understand, if you have to leave, you have to leave. I also realize that some of the above options are not cheap, but they are cheaper than home repairs and vet bills. Also, keep in mind that these options are only temporary solutions...assuming you follow the program laid out in detail on the previous pages. Remember, most of the solutions to separation anxiety have to do with how you behave when you are home with your dog.

CHAPTER 5 - SUMMARY

In a nutshell...

The biggest solution is to simply tell everyone in the house to stop giving the dog so much affection. Is it really that simple? Yes, in most cases it is exactly that simple.....or at least simple in theory. Simple doesn't always mean easy. It's absolutely not easy for most people to actually do it. As a matter of fact, some people will just straight out tell me they won't do it. Others will claim they are doing it but in fact they are not. As the saying goes, you can lead a horse to water but you can't make him drink. This book is the water; the rest is up to you.

There is a lot of detailed information in this book and it may not be a bad idea to read it more than once. However, you probably get the general idea and may just need some notes to look over for review or as you educate other family members, pet sitters and the like. Next, I've provided a brief recap of some of the key takeaways of the book.

As you may have noticed, the main theme of the book is centered around your behavior with your dog while you are actually home. If you get that in order, leaving the house will be a non-issue. So, rather than recap the entire book I am only going to provide an outline for the bulk of it, which is the first section of Chapter 4, entitled "When You Are Home" and is broken down into two parts. What follows is the bulleted version:

"Quick-View" Recap

Chapter 4 - Section 1 - When You Are Home
Part 1: Limited Affection and Attention

- Downplay Your Presence to Help Your Dog Deal with Your Absence
- Play Hard To Get
    - All attention on your terms/by invite only.
    - Ignore all demands for attention.
    - No eye contact.
    - The Walk Through
        - Walk through, not around, the dog.
        - Be careful to avoid injury.
    - Extinction and Extinction Burst
        - Behavior diminished through lacks of reinforcement.
        - May get worse before it gets better.
    - What You Pet Is What You Get.
- No Shadowing
    - No Hi, No Bye.
    - Come and go with no fanfare.
    - Close doors behind you.
    - The Walk Through
    - Tether, baby gates, crate, ex-pen, etc.
- No Dogs on the Furniture

- o   Creates small separation.
- o   Avoids too much affection.
- o   Get on floor for petting or cuddling.
- Use the Backyard or Car
  - o   Some dogs handle separation better in the yard or car.
  - o   No Hi, No Bye.
  - o   Call from other door *as last resort.*

Part 2: Unlimited Activities

- Exercise, Exercise, Exercise
  - o   To the point of exhaustion on a daily basis.
  - o   Structured daily walks are foundational.
    - ▪   Provides socialization and exercise.
    - ▪   Provides leadership and impulse control.
  - o   Must fulfill the dog's needs
    - ▪   What actually *is* enough, not what you think *should be* enough.
    - ▪   Most dogs require more than people suspect.
- Mental Exercise
  - o   Physical exercise alone may only create a super athlete prone to overstimulation.
  - o   Mental exercise also drains energy.

- Compare to a long day at the office or studying for school.
- Helps develop ability to relax.
  - Discipline and impulse control
    - Walking in Heel with no sniffing, pulling or lunging.
    - Controlled retrieves.
    - Obedience training.
  - The "Art of Doing Nothing"
    - Helps create calmness.
    - Non-active exercises such as long Down-Stays around distractions.
- Training Games
  - Must be totally under your control.
    - Train and maintain all rules.
    - Install an "on-off" switch.
  - "By invite only" rule still applies.
  - Incorporate some obedience exercises.
  - Don't let the dog be "Ball Crazy."
    - Engagement is good but obsession is a form of anxiety and stress.
    - One form of stress can lead to another.
- Obedience Training
  - Highly valuable to human-dog relationship.

- o   Helps establish authority and cross-species communication.
- o   Five basics of Heel, Sit, Down, Come and Stay.
- o   Focus on Stay and build up to a long Stay while you are out of sight.
- o   Go to Bed is another good one which is really just a Down-Stay with a send - off to a comfy location.
- Scent Games and Tricks
  - o   Teach dog to search for hidden treats and stuffed chew toys.
  - o   Work up to having the dog search unsupervised in the house or backyard.
  - o   Teach as many tricks as you want. It's good mental exercise and is a healthy way to give your dog attention that won't have a negative impact on separation anxiety.
- Use the backyard or go outside.
  - o   Give your dog affection, attention and play in the backyard as much as you like.
  - o   "By invite only" rule still applies, as always.
  - o   The backyard should be a happy place for your dog, not a place of banishment.

- Leadership
    - A good leader cares, first and foremost, for the well-being of his followers.
    - Nothing in Life is Free.
    - Learn to Earn.
    - Fulfill the dog's true needs.
    - Following the plan laid out in this book will build a lot of good leadership habits.
- Chew Toy Addiction
    - Stuffed Kong, raw bones, etc.
    - All meals can be stuffed in toys and fed in isolation area.
    - Can be had in your presence, at first. Once "addicted," the chew toy moves to isolation.
- Practice Isolation While You Are Home
    - Choose a safe area, preferably sound proof if you have a barker.
    - If using the backyard, warn your neighbors that there may be some barking.
    - *Pre-load* the isolation area
        - Use your dog's favorite extra-special-top-shelf-long-lasting treat that he is already addicted to.

- Treat should seem to have magically appeared or been brought by the Treat Fairy.
- Dog should now only get this special treat when in isolation, no longer in your presence.

o Enter and exit the isolation area calmly
- No Hi, No Bye.
- Practice your Wait command.
- End the isolation exercise before the dog has finished his treat. Reverse psychology will make him look forward to going in there again.
- Pick up the treat or leave it in the isolation area when the dog is not in there. Remember, he can only have it when alone.
- Never release the dog from his isolation area if he is whining, scratching, barking, etc.
- Once released from the area, continue to ignore for a few minutes or until calm and away from you.
- Start with short durations and gradually build up to longer and longer durations.

- What About the Barking?
  - ○ Don't commit to the isolation area until you have already dealt with shadowing and affection issues outlined previously. This will minimize the likelihood and intensity of barking.
  - ○ Extinction - ignoring is your first line of defense. Once in the area you are committed to waiting for calm and quiet. Do not release from the area or give attention while barking, whining, etc.
  - ○ Extinction Burst - don't be surprised if it gets worse before it gets better. Don't give in.
  - ○ If using the backyard, you can call from another door or go around to the gate, BUT only as a last resort. Don't let the dog realize that barking at the back door makes you go around to the side door.
- What About Punishment?
  - ○ *The name of the game with separation anxiety is desensitization and counter-conditioning rather than punishment.*
  - ○ As a general rule, punishment is a bad idea for separation anxiety.
    - ▪ The dog is already in a state of fear or panic, so punishment

> may cause more fear and subsequently worsen the anxiety.
- Barking is not the problem, it's a symptom of the problem, hence the holistic nature of this book.
- Attempts at punishment can also be interpreted as a reward because the dog is getting attention.

o Sometimes mild corrections can be effective and beneficial but this is risky.
- Emphasis on the words *sometimes* and *mild*. We are not opening the door for abuse here.
- If a quick firm tone of voice or maybe a loud hand clap or foot stomp gets the dog to quiet down then that's fine, but this is rarely the case. Most people have already tried this and if it worked they wouldn't be reading this book or calling me for help.

o Critical Questions: Has the dog been trained with corrections or only positive reinforcement? Has the dog been exposed to traumatizing or abusive forms of punishment? Has he been previously taught a "Quiet" command of some sort?

- If he has not been taught to be quiet previously, then don't try to teach during a meltdown.
- If he has never been trained in a firm manner or has been abused, yelling at him during a separation episode is a bad move and pretty much guaranteed to make it worse.

o Teaching "Quiet!" or "No!" or any other negative commands should be done outside of a separation anxiety meltdown.

- Train these things at another time and place. Only then can they be helpful.
- Should be part of a basic communication system, not something scary or traumatizing.

o Training with any sort of physical pressure or corrections should be *layered* into your training by balancing with plenty of positive reinforcement and in scenarios that do not affect separation anxiety.

- A light leash pop to gain attention followed by praise, petting and a treat, for example.
- Out on a walk or in an obedience class might be appropriate times to introduce these concepts to your repertoire.
  - *Hiring a balanced professional trainer/behaviorist is highly recommended before attempting any punishment on your own.*
- Look for Triggers
  - A trigger is anything that signals the dog you are going to leave such as blow drying your hair, grabbing your keys or putting on your nice shoes.
  - Once you've identified the triggers, you must desensitize your dog to them. Pick up your keys and walk around the house with them but don't leave, for example.
- Have Your Dog Bond With Other People
  - If the dog is only anxious when apart from one person, have her bond with other friends or family members.
  - Let the others feed, walk and play with the dog while you continue to play hard to get.

So that's the short version of what I believe are the most important parts of the book. Once these things are in order you can simply start leaving the house in small increments as laid out in the rest of Chapter 4. Please don't use this as a replacement for actually reading the book. It is only meant to be a quick reference for reminders after you have actually read the book in its entirety. Below are a couple closing notes and words of encouragement.

Be Consistent. To be effective, this program must be practiced every day by every family member. If three out of the four family members are not giving too much affection to the dog but the other member (because they feel guilty) is making up for lost hugs and kisses, this program won't be as successful. Be sure to get the whole family on board. Let them all read this book as a way to get on the same page.

Feel Good About It. Be confident and know that this program will help your dog to stop his suffering. Trust me, your dog doesn't enjoy feeling anxious, so these steps are actually the most affectionate thing you can do.

Don't Be Afraid To Ask For Help. Please keep in mind that no book will ever replace personalized training from a qualified professional, so don't hesitate to contact and interview some trainers in your area if you continue to have problems after implementing the strategies put forth by this book.

ABOUT THE AUTHOR

Chad Culp, CDT is a graduate of Animal Behavior College and Global College of Natural Medicine. Chad is a Certified Dog Trainer, Canine Behavior Specialist, Canine Nutrition Consultant, author, radio show host, and world-wide dog advice persona. Chad owns and operates Thriving Canine, a worldwide, full-service dog training and behavior platform.

Chad offers private training in the California Bay Area and phone or video consults for those with dog training questions or canine behavior issues in other parts of the world.

See www.ThrivingCanine.com for tons of free information.

Made in the USA
San Bernardino, CA
09 February 2017